being a pro
footballer

Sarah Levete

Published in 2013 by Wayland

Copyright © Wayland 2013

Wayland
Hachette Children's Books
338 Euston Road
London NW1 3BH

Wayland Australia
Level 17/207 Kent Street
Sydney NSW 2000

Concept by Joyce Bentley

Commissioned by Debbie Foy and
Rasha Elsaeed

Produced for Wayland by Calcium
Designer: Paul Myerscough
Editor: Sarah Eason

British Library Cataloguing in Publication Data

Being a pro footballer. — (Top jobs)(Radar)
   1. Soccer players—Juvenile literature.
   2. Professional sports—Juvenile literature.
   I. Series
   796.3'34'092-dc23

ISBN: 978 0 7502 7848 5

Every effort has been made to clear copyright.
Should there be any inadvertent omission, please
apply to the publisher for rectification.

Printed in China

0 9 8 7 6 5 4 3 2 1

Wayland is a division of Hachette Children's Books,
an Hachette UK company.

www.hachette.co.uk

Acknowledgements: Dreamstime: Galina Barskaya
26t; Getty Images: AFP 12–13; Rex Features: Eallen/
Daily Mail 28; Shutterstock: Lucian Coman 11t,
creativedoxfoto 22–23, De Visu 19t, Andreas Gradin
2–3, Cyril Hou 19b, Jaggat 10r, 16bl, Aptyp Kok 2t, 6,
John Lumb 10bl, Eoghan McNally 30b, Natursports
5l, 10tl, 18, Sportgraphic cover, 1, 2b, 9, 11b, 24, 29,
30–31, Sportsphotographer.eu 19c, Laszlo Szirtesi 20b,
Matt Trommer 20–21, Lario Tus 4–5, 26–27, Rob Wilson
3br, Ahmad Faizal Yahya 2c, 14b, 16–17, 16bc, 16br;
Wikipedia: David Herrmann 15r.

cover stories

the**people**

the**moves**

the**talk**

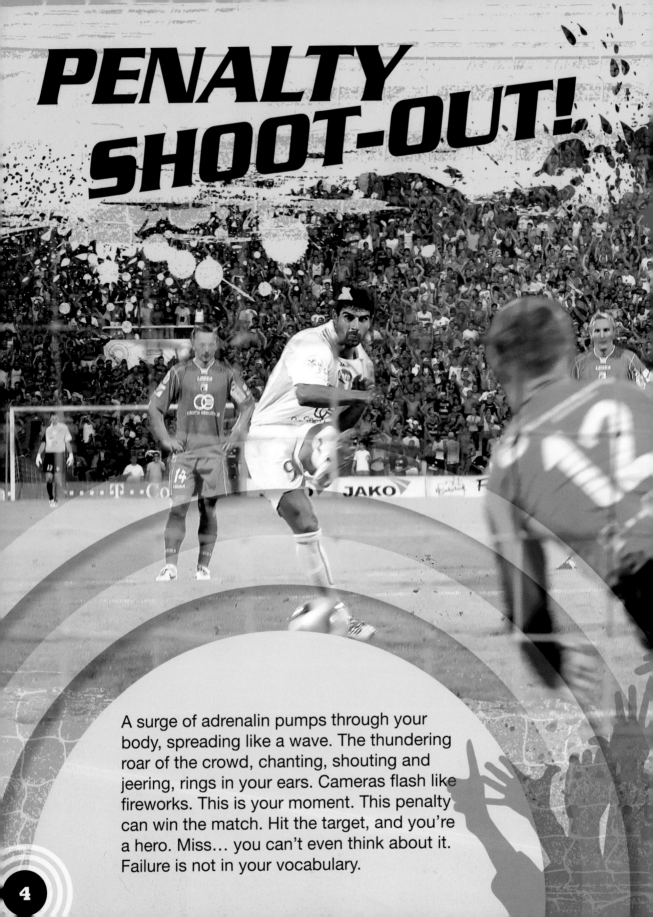

PENALTY SHOOT-OUT!

A surge of adrenalin pumps through your body, spreading like a wave. The thundering roar of the crowd, chanting, shouting and jeering, rings in your ears. Cameras flash like fireworks. This is your moment. This penalty can win the match. Hit the target, and you're a hero. Miss… you can't even think about it. Failure is not in your vocabulary.

Focus

There is just time to focus and let the hum of the fans' noise fizzle out like swirls of smoke. You must block out the TV cameras and the clicking photographers and just do it – forgetting the millions of eyes in the stadium and around the world intently watching your every move.

In position

You place the ball on the penalty spot, look around and get into position. The goalkeeper scans your body and face for clues, trying to work out where you will aim. He is as desperate to save the goal as you are to score it.

Kick!

The referee's whistle pierces through the silence in your mind. The force of your kick smashes through the ball. All eyes are tracking the ball's flight, watching it curve through the air, just beyond the goalkeeper's reach to land in the back of the net. The goal – and match – is yours!

FOOTBALL DREAM

My story by Melchi Emanuel-Williamson

I started playing football at the age of seven for a local Sunday league club. A coach thought I had potential, so he took me to play in a tournament with a leading London club's under-eights team. The club invited me for a six-week trial but signed me after one game. I was amazed.

I trained for about two hours, up to three times a week, and there was usually a match at the weekend, too. My family was brilliant. My parents drove me all over the country for matches and encouraged me to keep going when I was off with injuries or wasn't selected for a match. They even came with me to Italy to play the under-nines at AC Milan and Inter Milan – that was a fantastic experience!

It's been hard keeping up with friends as well as training, but I realise now it could be worth it if I achieve my dream of becoming a professional footballer. It's not been easy fitting in homework and training, especially when I need to revise for exams. But it's important to have something to fall back on – just in case I don't make it as a professional footballer. When I had some injury problems with my ankles, it made me realise how uncertain a footballer's career can be.

I've got a few trials with clubs coming up, so now I'm just waiting for the right club to offer me a contract. I may not be what one club is looking for, but I just might be perfect for another.

The hard work and the sacrifices are worth it because I love the game and I love playing – and that's why I'm determined to make it.

Top professional footballers are highly skilled and well-paid athletes. Some players, such as Cristiano Ronaldo and Lionel Messi, can earn up to £100,000 – in just one week! However, research shows it can take an incredible 10,000 hours of practice over ten years to make it to the top. Even then, it can be a long, tough journey to stay there.

TURNING PRO

Spotted!

The managers of local or school teams often tip-off scouts (talent spotters) about a particularly gifted player. Sometimes, a scout from a club just turns up to watch a game. If players are scouted, they usually have a trial with the club. The coach talks to the players and watches them before deciding whether or not to sign them. Young players work their way up through the club's teams until they are 16 years old.

A tough profession

When they reach the age of 16, many players who have trained hard with a club will not make it to the professional level. The club 'releases' them if coaches do not think they will make it to the top. Only a handful of hopefuls are offered professional contracts. Even then, they may not find a place in the club's first team.

Life as a pro

Professional football is competitive and ruthless. The rewards for a top-level professional are great, but the risks are huge. Footballers can suddenly find themselves out of the game with an injury or replaced by another player. To stay on the pitch rather than the bench, every pro must train incredibly hard. It is crucial that players stay in peak physical condition and give their best performance in every match.

FOOTBALL FIT

Sprinting drills during training sesssions and before matches prepare players' bodies for the demanding bursts of energy required during play.

Stretching is an essential part of training – a muscle injury can put a player out of action for weeks or even months.

Ladder jumps help to develop the super-fast reflexes a player needs to respond to the opposition's moves during play.

Professional football teams are supported by a group of therapists, including masseurs, to ensure they stay in match fit shape.

Players drink specially-formulated sports drinks throughout training and during matches to replace lost fluid, salt and minerals.

Being a professional footballer is not just about talent. Any player who wants to stay in the game must keep their fitness levels to the maximum – players can spend more than 90 minutes sprinting up and down the pitch. The club's doctor has the final word on who is match fit. Without his or her approval, a player will be on the bench.

Speed and stamina

Coaches work out training programmes to develop the skills, techniques and fitness every player needs. Hopping, jumping and sprinting drills help to keep up speed and stamina. For lightning-quick reflexes, players train on the ladder jump, running and jumping through the rungs of a flat training ladder laid out on the ground.

Stop start

During a match, footballers race down the pitch, suddenly stop to kick the ball, and then speed off again. To improve stamina for these explosive bursts of energy, players practise running a set distance as fast as possible before an alarm sounds. Every time they repeat the exercise, the alarm bleeps earlier. To improve agility and footwork, players practise leaping onto a raised platform, landing as lightly as possible and leaping off, again landing lightly.

Avoiding injury

Players perform stretches before and after training or matches to try to avoid tearing a muscle. After intense training and exhausting matches, a physiotherapist helps to ease players' aches and pains and ensures the correct treatment is given for injuries. They also use massage, stretches and exercises to keep players match fit.

Food is fuel

Players follow a well-planned diet for top performances. Carbohydrates from foods such as pasta, oats and potatoes slowly release energy, while protein from foods such as meat, fish and pulses helps the build-up and recovery of muscles.

MARTA

THE STATS

Name: Marta Vieira da Silva
Born: 19 February 1986
Place of birth: Dois
Riachos, Brazil
Nationality: Brazilian
Job: Professional footballer

New beginnings

When she was 14 years old, Marta took a bus to Rio de Janeiro to try out for Vasco da Gama football club's girls' team. From that moment, her life changed. She made it into the team and stayed with the Brazilian club for four years.

Beating the boys

Passionate about playing football, Marta spent much of her childhood kicking a ball around in her Brazilian hometown. Despite jeers from young boys who did not think football was a girl's game, Marta often outpaced and outperformed the boys.

Going stateside

In 2009, Marta gained more fans and more fame when she moved to the USA to play for clubs Los Angeles Sol and then Gold Pride. Her determination and skills helped Gold Pride win the 2010 Women's Professional Soccer Championship.

Goal maker!

At the age of 18, Marta headed for Sweden, which had a well-established women's league. There, she joined the club Umeå IK and her career took off. In just four years, she had scored an outstanding 111 goals in 103 games.

Top of her game

Wherever Marta plays, she has won awards and fans. She is the only professional footballer, male or female, to have won FIFA's World Player of the Year/Ballon d'Or award for five years in a row (2006–2010). Nicknamed 'Pelé with skirts', Marta explodes through the opposition on the pitch. Her skills, passion and energy mark her out as one of the best professional football players in the world. She is also a Goodwill Ambassador for the United Nations Development Programme (UNDP) to help women around the world fight poverty.

PITCH TALK

Sound like a pro on the pitch with Radar's guide to footie jargon.

bench
where substitutes sit as they wait to come onto the pitch

cap
to make an appearance for a national team. Actual caps are sometimes given to players

Champions League
a cup competition organised by the Union of European Football Associations (UEFA) for the top football clubs in Europe

chip
a kick where the ball travels in an arc through the air

dribble
to tap and nudge the ball down the pitch, keeping control and possession of the ball

drills
exercises done over and over to perfect certain skills or to improve fitness

dummy
to pretend to move one way to trick another player

first team
a club's first choice of players plus 11 substitutes

formation
the way the team is organised on the pitch

friendly
match that is not part of an organised competition or tournament

hat-trick
when a player scores three goals in a match

kick-off
the start of a football match

La Liga
the top football league for Spanish teams

league
a set number of teams that compete against each other

league club
a club in one of a country's top professional leagues

match fit
to be declared fit enough to play in a game

penalty kick
a kick awarded to the opposition for a foul in the penalty area

released
being let go from a contract

replica kit
kit that looks exactly like that of a particular professional team, such as Liverpool FC

drills

scout
a person whose job it is to spot talented footballers

sign
to give a player a contract (either as a youth player or professional)

sponsorship
to give money to a club or player in return for advertising and displaying a brand or company name on kit or other club equipment

strip
the clothing worn by a team

sub
short for substitute, a player who does not start the game, but comes onto the pitch to replace a tired or injured player, or to change the team's formation and tactics

suspension
not allowed to play in a match

transfer fee
the money paid by one club to another in order to buy a player

trial
a try-out with a club over one session or several weeks

Some teams change the design of their strips each football season.

GLOSSARY

adrenalin
a hormone found in the human body that causes the heart to beat faster and gives a 'rushing' feeling

agent
a person paid to get the best deals for a player

agility
moving quickly and smoothly

dehydration
not having enough fluid in the body

drugs test
a urine test to check a player has not used illegal substances to improve his or her performance

media
press, such as newspapers, radio, TV and the internet

merchandise
goods, such as hats, scarves and replica kit, which bear a club's logo or badge

physiotherapist
a specialist who works on muscles in the body to relieve pain

potential
to have a talent that can be developed

pro
short for professional. A professional footballer is paid to play the game

reflexes
spontaneous reactions of the muscles

stamina
to be able to do physical exercise over a long period of time

strategy
a plan to win a game

visualisation
creating images of something in your mind

15

GARY NEVILLE

Radar consultant Gary Neville has been a professional player at his favourite club, Manchester United, for the whole of his career. We asked the veteran defender about his dream job.

What makes a top player?

Practice and natural talent are essential. You also need a bit of luck and to be injury free to have a chance.

How long did you train in a typical day?

Pre-season it would be two hours twice a day. During the season with matches every three days, it would be once for one hour and 30 minutes. The day before a game would be one hour and after the game we'd warm down for 45 minutes.

Are there any football skills you find difficult – if so, which ones?

Quite a few! Dribbling, shooting, scoring, playing with my back to play, they're all difficult and the reason why I was a defender for the whole of my career. I don't know any defender who wouldn't swap if he could score 20 goals a season or dribble and beat players with the ball at his feet.

How do you keep going when you're two goals down?

You have to have an inbuilt willingness to go to the last minute of every match, whatever the score. If you are 2–0 down and you can get one goal back, the other team can easily become nervous and start to panic. So many games can change in one moment, so you just keep going.

What was the worst moment in your career?

Getting injured against Bolton Wanderers in March 2007. It is a sportsman's worst fear when his career is taken out of his hands.

What is a typical pre-match meal?

Mine was spaghetti with a small spoon of tomato sauce and fruit squash. Other players eat chicken, salad, soup, salmon and lots of vegetables. All low-fat things.

What was the best moment in your career?

Playing my debut for Manchester United. It was the realisation of a dream. I had supported the club since the age of five and it was all I ever wanted to do. In this one three-minute appearance I knew that no-one could take my dream away from me.

What's the best advice for someone who wants to be a professional footballer?

If you give the very best that you can in every way, then there isn't much else you can do!

SUPER SALARIED?

YES

With some professional footballers earning up to £100,000 a week, many people believe that players are overpaid. They argue that:

1. Young footballers often cannot handle the fame and attention that comes with earning so much money and they end up facing personal and professional problems.
2. The lifestyle professional players can afford to enjoy can distract them from training and can make them lose focus.
3. Paying players such high wages means that fans have to pay more to watch the games live.
4. Pay should be more equal between male and female players. Clubs should lower male players' wages and use some of the money to pay women footballers a better wage.
5. Small clubs will never be able to compete with the wealthiest clubs, which can afford to pay the highest wages. This means smaller clubs find it hard to attract the best players and rarely move up the league.
6. Footballers just kick a ball around a pitch. Doctors, nurses and fire fighters who save lives should earn more.

On the other side of the argument, many people believe that footballers' wages reflect their brilliance and expertise on the pitch. They make the point that:

1. Top footballers deserve high wages because their playing days are limited (most retire when they reach their 30s) and they run the risk of injury ruining their careers.
2. Top actors and other sports people, such as golfers and racing drivers, are often paid as much as footballers, so it seems unfair to single out footballers.
3. The highest paid footballers are some of the most talented people in the world – their pay should reflect this.
4. The money spent on top footballers is earned back by clubs through selling tickets for matches, merchandise such as replica kit, and selling TV companies the rights to show the matches.
5. Football is one of the most-watched sports in the world. Footballers provide lots of entertainment for people, so why shouldn't they earn a lot?

NO

RIGHT OR WRONG?

Football is a global, billion-pound industry. Some top footballers earn more than prime ministers and presidents but they attract many fans to the game. It is up to clubs to decide how much to pay them. However, a limit on footballers' pay could mean that smaller clubs would be able to afford the best players and it would be easier for those clubs to move up in the league.

PRO MOVES

Dribble or dummy, every pro has perfected some key moves to shape a game. It is fun to watch fancy footwork, and these skills also confuse and outwit opponents.

1. The Cruyff turn

Dutch player Johan Cruyff perfected this tricky move. The player looks to pass the ball, but instead, uses the inside foot of the kicking leg to drag the ball behind the standing leg. The player turns the shoulders in line with the ball and dribbles away in another direction, leaving the defender confused and out-played.

Type 'Match Magazine – FA skills – how to do the Cruyff turn' and 'flip flap soccer trick' into www.youtube.com to see these pro moves in action.

2. Flip flap

This move looks simple, but it takes a long time to perfect. It was made famous by the Brazilian player Roberto Rivelino and then more recently by Ronaldinho. In this move, the player flicks the ball with the outside of the foot and then quickly flicks it back in the opposite direction by tapping it back with the inside of the same foot.

Type 'Pelé bicycle kick' and 'René Higuita scorpion kick' into www.youtube.com to see the masters perform these moves.

4. Bicycle kick

This is a dangerous move! Brazilian footballer Pelé first wowed the crowds with this acrobatic bicycle kick, which lifted him off the ground and allowed him to shoot backwards while airborne! In this move, the player throws him or herself off the ground and uses a pedalling movement to keep in the air, at the same time as kicking the ball, before landing safely on the ground.

5. Rabona

From England's Joe Cole to Portugal's Cristiano Ronaldo, top football players use the rabona to surprise their opponents. The player kicks the ball with one leg wrapped around the other. Right-footed players cross the right foot behind the left to chip the ball with the right; left-footed players cross the left foot behind the right.

3. Scorpion

Colombian goalkeeper René Higuita turned goalkeeping upside down with the scorpion kick. The keeper lets the ball go over the head, but then dives forward to kick it away with both heels. It is a risky move because if the timing is wrong, the ball will go in the net.

Type 'FIFA 11 – rabona kick tutorial' into www.youtube.com to watch this move.

FOOTY FACTS

36

The number of red cards in one match shown to players, subs and coaches. It was played in 2011 between the two Argentinian clubs Claypole and Victoriano Arenas.

£80 MILLION

The highest transfer fee ever paid for a footballer – paid to Manchester United for Cristiano Ronaldo by Real Madrid in 2009.

352

The record-breaking number of caps given to USA's Kristine Lilly.

13

The most goals scored in an international match by a single player (Australia's Archie Thompson against American Samoa).

£25 MILLION

Messi's approximate earnings in one year from his club (FC Barcelona), advertising and sponsorship deals.

105,000

The total number of spectators that can fit inside Mexico's Estadio Azteca, one of the world's largest football stadiums.

158

Female professional footballer Mia Hamm's record-winning number of goals in international matches for the USA.

10
KILOMETRES

The approximate distance covered by a professional midfield player during a match.

£30.9
MILLION

The value of Manchester United's previous sponsorship deal with sports manufacturer Nike. This is being renegotiated in 2013, and is widely expected to be the richest kit deal in the history of football.

600

The number of pairs of football boots the England squad took to the 2010 World Cup.

LIONEL MESSI

LEFT-FOOTED LEGEND

THE STATS
Name: Lionel Messi
Born: 24 June 1987
Place of birth: Rosario, Argentina
Club: FC Barcelona

Lionel Messi is considered one of the most highly skilled footballers of his generation.

Early starter

When he was five years old, Messi began training with a local club where his father was the coach. By the age of eight, Messi's talent was obvious and he joined the Argentinian football academy called Newell's Old Boys. Messi was clearly a player to watch but he suffered from a medical condition that meant that his growth and development was delayed. The regular medical treatment needed for the problem was too expensive for Argentinian clubs. It looked as if Messi's career would never take off.

Messi moves

Messi's luck changed, aged 13, when he caught the eye of scouts for the Spanish team FC Barcelona (known as Barca). The club offered to pay for his medical treatment, but it meant Messi would need to move to Spain. Messi and his family left Argentina so he could play for Barcelona's youth team. He quickly impressed the coaches, and at just 16 years old, he was on the pitch with Barcelona's first team.

World stage

Messi's magic helped his national team win the Under-20 World Cup in 2004. However, Messi's next international performance in 2005 was not his best – after just 40 seconds of play he left the pitch in tears, sent off for elbowing another player.

Magic touch

The nimble Messi was not down for long and soon became an international football star. Since 2006, he has won awards and broken records, including becoming the youngest Barcelona player to score 100 goals. He is also Barca's highest goalscorer in a single season – 53 in 2010/11 – breaking Ronaldo's previous record of 47. Superstar Messi has helped Barca win the Champions League and La Liga competitions and continues to shine on the pitch, delighting fans with his left-footed brilliance.

Career highlights

2006 2007 2008 2009 World Soccer Player of the Year

2007 scored a hat-trick against rival team Real Madrid

2009/2010 2010/2011 UEFA Champions League Top Scorer

2009-2012 FIFA World Player of the Year/Ballon d'Or

2011 Player of the Year in Europe

A PROFESSIONAL PLAYER ON LIFE ON AND OFF THE PITCH

MATCH DAY

SATURDAY MARCH 26, 2011

8am If it's an away game, I usually wake up in my hotel bedroom, where we stay the night before to ensure we get enough rest and relaxation before the game. Breakfast is cereal, toast, juice and a banana.

10am Before the match, the doctor checks everyone is match fit. It's stressful if you've had an injury and you're waiting for the go ahead to play. But if you play with an injury, you could be out all season. We will have tried out the formation before match day and we'll all know the game plan after intensive practice sessions. Before a big game, we also watch the other team's matches so we know exactly what we need to do to outplay them.

12pm I eat a light lunch – maybe pasta and sauce – before a match and then try to have some chill-out time to relax my mind and keep me fresh for the kick-off. On match day, it's time to put visualisation and focusing exercises into practice to keep a clear head. It's important to make sure you don't get dehydrated on the pitch. You sweat out so much water and dehydration really saps your energy. We are weighed before and after a match because that shows you how much fluid you lose during a game. Then you can make sure you drink enough afterwards to replace it.

1.30pm At the ground, some players have a massage as part of their warm-up. Other players are a bit superstitious and always go through the same routine before a game for luck. When everyone is ready, the manager comes in and gives a bit of a talk or wishes us luck.

3.00pm Let the game begin... Kick-off time!

About 5pm After the match, TV reporters often ask us for interviews. We have all had media training to help us with these because they can be tricky, especially if your team hasn't played as well as it could have.

Some players take an icy bath to help their muscles recover from the intense exercise, but I prefer a massage. I have a sports drink and an energy bar to help me regain my energy quickly. It's important to eat carbohydrates after a match to replace lost energy, and protein to help muscles recover. We hand over our kit to the kit manager who makes sure it's ready for the next match. There's usually a post-match analysis to look at what went well and what went wrong — and then the coach uses that in the next training session.

6:30pm On the coach home, it's quite a chilled-out mood — all depending on the result of course. Not so chilled if bad!

9pm When I get home, I just like to relax with my family and enjoy an early night. Match day is stressful, so it's good to unwind.

THE BEAUTIFUL GAME

People have been playing football for centuries, but the game has come a long way from its beginnings. According to legend, in medieval times people kicked around pigs' bladders to score points against opposition teams!

Billy Wright (above right, 1924–1994) was the first football player in the world to play for his country 100 times. He made 105 appearances for England, and was captain a record 90 times.

Professional football

The first football club was founded in Sheffield, England, in 1857. Soon many more clubs formed and in 1885, the English Football Association allowed clubs to start paying players. Before then, some lucky players received unofficial 'boot money' – extra money put in their football boots!

New times, new rules

Before 1961, the most footballers could earn was £20 a week (now worth about £340)! Even when that rule changed in 1961, the amount footballers earned was still tiny compared to today. Footballers were 'owned' by clubs who could keep a player even if he wanted to move to another club. The rules changed during the 1960s and it became easier for footballers to transfer from one club to another and also from one country to another.

Going global

In the 1990s, TV companies started to pay huge amounts of money to football organisations to show matches worldwide. Businesses realised the value of paying clubs to display their logos on kit and in the stadium, and football soon evolved into a multi-billion pound global business.

Money, money, money

Today, top footballers' pay has soared – Argentinian player Carlos Tévez is reported to earn more than £600,000 a month. Competition between clubs is stiff, so professional footballers employ agents to negotiate the best deals and to fix up lucrative sponsorship opportunities that earn them millions of pounds on top of their pay packets. These days, the best footballers have become top celebrities who can earn huge amounts of money by advertising food or even just by turning up to the opening of a new restaurant.

Women's football

During the First World War (1914–1918) when many men were away fighting, women's football became a real crowd-puller, with tens of thousands of people watching games. Yet today, women's football does not get the same media attention as men's football, and women fight for the right to be fully professional. Some of the best-established women's teams in the world include Norway, Japan, Germany and the USA.

Today, football clubs fight to gain ownership of star players such as Tévez.

A TEAM EFFORT

Behind every successful player there's a hard-working team, from the people who keep the kit in good condition to the nutritionist who advises players about diet. When the England players travelled to South Africa for the 2010 World Cup, they were supported by a back-room team of 35!

The boss

The manager agrees transfer deals and loans, and works closely with the coach to decide who is in the team and who is on the bench. Together with the first team coach, the manager discusses and decides on the team's formation and strategy for important games. There are often coaches that work with specific players, for example the defence coach will work mainly with the backs, while the goalkeeping coach will train the goalkeeper.

The skipper

The club captain of a football team, sometimes known as the skipper, is a squad member chosen to be the spokesperson for the players: it is often one of the older or more experienced members of the squad, or a player that can heavily influence a game. If the club captain cannot play in a match, a team captain is chosen and is usually identified by the wearing of an armband.

Psychologists

Top clubs use sports psychologists to help players develop the best attitude for success. They help them to focus on the game, blocking out any distractions. Players are taught to imagine success, to visualise saving the goal or getting it in the net. Psychologists help players manage their moods because an outburst on the pitch can result in a red card and suspension. They also help players to rebuild their confidence after a long break due to injury or after a missed tackle or penalty.

Team managers, such as Barcelona's Josep Guardiola, direct their players during matches to get the best possible performance from the team.

The food coach

A nutritionist or food scientist advises players on what to eat to give them maximum energy and fitness. The nutritionist also advises on what not to eat and drink because some common energy drinks and foods contain substances that may give a false positive result in a drugs test.

KICK START

Scouts say that if you are a talented player, they will find you! So what are you waiting for? Join a local club or the school team and kick-off your football career!

People to talk to

The Football Association's website features lots of information on ways to get into football from playing to coaching:
www.thefa.com/getintofootball

Find out more about women's football and how you could be the next star player at:
www.shekicks.net
www.womenssoccerunited.com

Get the latest tips and training techniques with photos and videos of skills at:
http://expertfootball.com
www.talkfootball.co.uk

Reads & Apps

There are some great books that can tell you more about professional football:

FIFA World Football Records
by Keir Radnedge (Carlton Books, 2011)

Celebrity Secrets: Footballers
by Adam Sutherland (Wayland, 2012)

Football Focus (series of four books)
by Clive Gifford (Wayland, 2009)

Download *Flick Kick Football* or *Flick Soccer!* to see if you can cut it as a pro striker. Choose your team and play to win with *FIFA 11*. All three apps are available from:
www.itunes.com
https://market.android.com

INDEX